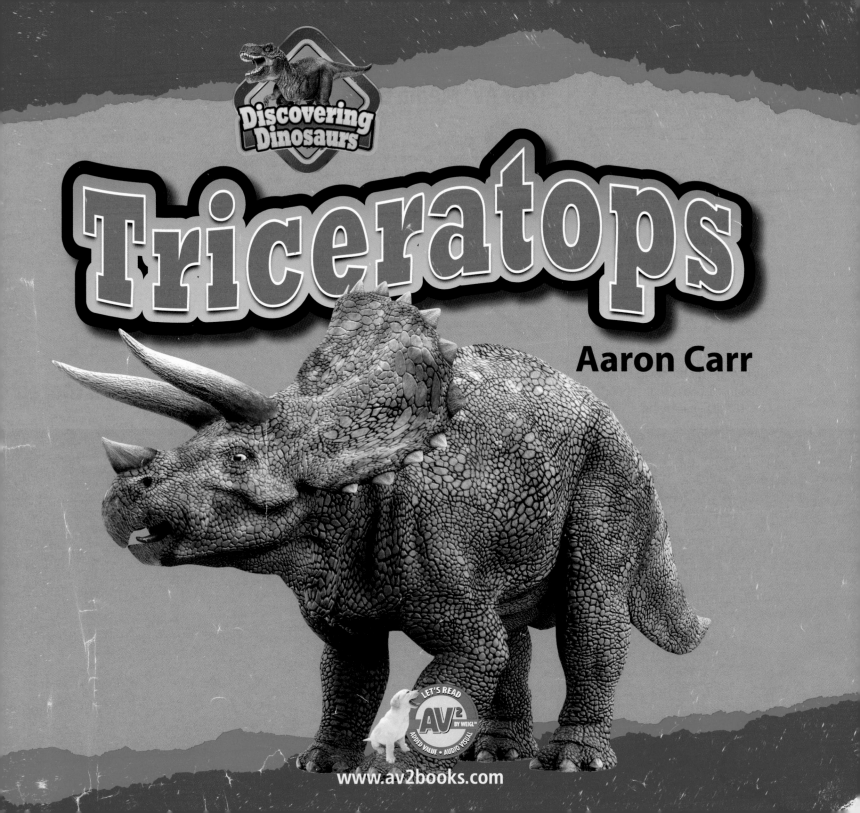

Discovering Dinosaurs

Triceratops

Aaron Carr

LET'S READ

AV²
BY WEIGL™

ADDED VALUE • AUDIO VISUAL

Go to **www.av2books.com**, and enter this book's unique code.

BOOK CODE

B673065

AV² by Weigl brings you media enhanced books that support active learning.

AV² provides enriched content that supplements and complements this book. Weigl's AV² books strive to create inspired learning and engage young minds in a total learning experience.

Your AV² Media Enhanced books come alive with...

Audio
Listen to sections of the book read aloud.

Video
Watch informative video clips.

Embedded Weblinks
Gain additional information for research.

Try This!
Complete activities and hands-on experiments.

Key Words
Study vocabulary, and complete a matching word activity.

Quizzes
Test your knowledge.

Slide Show
View images and captions, and prepare a presentation.

... and much, much more!

Published by AV² by Weigl
350 5th Avenue, 59th Floor New York, NY 10118
Website: www.av2books.com   www.weigl.com

Library of Congress Control Number: 2013937451
ISBN 978-1-62127-241-0 (hardcover)
ISBN 978-1-62127-247-2 (softcover)

Printed in the United States of America in North Mankato, Minnesota
2 3 4 5 6 7 8 9 0 17 16 15 14 13

112013
WEP111113

Project Coordinator: Aaron Carr   Art Director: Terry Paulhus

All illustrations by Jon Hughes, pixel-shack.com; Getty Images: 19 inset; Alamy: 20.

Triceratops

In this book,
you will learn

what its
name means

what it
looked like

where it lived

what it ate

and much more!

Meet the Triceratops.
Its name means
"three-horned face."

Triceratops had two long horns and one short horn.

Its two big horns
were three feet long.

Triceratops had the largest head of any animal that has ever lived on land.

Its head could be six feet wide
and eight feet long.

Triceratops was a plant eater.

10

It ate plants
that grew along the ground.

Triceratops had a mouth
shaped like a beak.
It used its beak-shaped mouth
to rip apart its food.

13

Triceratops moved slowly on four short legs.

Its front legs were shorter than its back legs.

Triceratops lived
near lakes and ponds.

It lived in the west part of North America.

17

Triceratops died out more than 65 million years ago.

People learned about Triceratops from fossils.

People can go to museums to see fossils and learn more about the Triceratops.

DINOSAUR

21

Triceratops Facts

These pages provide detailed information that expands on the interesting facts found in the book. They are intended to be used by adults as a learning support to help young readers round out their knowledge of each amazing dinosaur or pterosaur featured in the *Discovering Dinosaurs* series.

Pages 4–5

Triceratops means "three-horned face." The Triceratops was a large dinosaur best known for having three horns on its head. It had a stocky, powerful body similar to the modern-day rhinoceros. A Triceratops could be up to 30 feet (9 meters) long and 10 feet (3 m) tall and may have weighed as much as 26,000 pounds (11,800 kilograms).

Pages 6–7

Triceratops had two long horns and one short horn. Measuring more than 3 feet (1 m) long, the long horns were located above the Triceratops' eyes. The short horn was above its mouth. Most scientists believe the Triceratops used its horn to defend itself from predators, such as the Tyrannosaurus rex. The horns may have also been used to attract mates.

Pages 8–9

Triceratops had the largest head of any land animal. The Triceratops also had a bony plate, called a frill, on its head. The frill could be up to 6 feet (1.8 m) wide and had a line of spikes along its outside edge. Scientists are not sure how the Triceratops used the frill. It may have protected the Triceratops' neck from predators, or it may have been used to attract mates. The frill developed holes as the Triceratops grew older, so it may have also helped in determining age.

Pages 10–11

Triceratops was a herbivore, or plant-eater. The Triceratops ate a wide variety of low-lying plants, such as shrubs and cycads. Unlike most other herbivorous dinosaurs, the Triceratops could eat tough, woody plants as well as softer, green plants. This gave the Triceratops an advantage over many other dinosaurs. For this reason, the Triceratops was the most dominant herbivore of its time.

Pages 12–13

Triceratops had a beak-shaped mouth. Scientists believe the shape of the mouth, combined with its powerful jaws, helped the Triceratops to cut through or grasp its food. To help chew its food, the Triceratops had hundreds of teeth. The teeth were arranged in many columns that lined the cheeks. The Triceratops could have as many as 800 teeth, though only a small number of these were used at any one time.

Pages 14–15

Triceratops had four short legs. The Triceratops had thick, strong hind legs and slightly shorter front legs. This made the Triceratops appear to lean forward slightly. Evidence from fossilized dinosaur tracks suggest that the Triceratops walked in a manner similar to modern-day large mammals, such as elephants. Though the Triceratops had powerful legs, it likely could not move very quickly.

Pages 16–17

Triceratops lived in the western part of North America. The Triceratops lived in lush areas throughout the western parts of what is now the United States and Canada. As a herbivore, the Triceratops had to live near vegetation. It preferred forested areas near lakes and ponds. Many scientists believe the Triceratops lived in herds with many other members of its species.

Pages 18–19

Triceratops lived more than 65 million years ago during the Late Cretaceous Period. This period ended with a meteor impact that led to the extinction of the dinosaurs. All that people know about the Triceratops comes from studying fossils. Fossils form when an animal dies and is covered in sand, mud, or water. This keeps the hard parts of the body, such as bones, teeth, and claws, from decomposing. The body is pressed between layers of mud and sand. Over millions of years, the layers turn into stone, and the dinosaur's bones and teeth turn into stone as well. This preserves the size and shape of the dinosaur.

Pages 20–21

People can go to museums to see fossils and learn more about the Triceratops. People from all around the world visit museums each year to see Triceratops fossils in person. Not many Triceratops fossils have been found, and most of those are not complete. This means most museums display replicas of Triceratops fossils. However, the Children's Museum in Indiana is home to Kelsey, one of the most complete Triceratops fossils in the world.

KEY WORDS

Research has shown that as much as 65 percent of all written material published in English is made up of 300 words. These 300 words cannot be taught using pictures or learned by sounding them out. They must be recognized by sight. This book contains 51 common sight words to help young readers improve their reading fluency and comprehension. This book also teaches young readers several important content words, such as proper nouns. These words are paired with pictures to aid in learning and improve understanding.

Page	Sight Words First Appearance
5	face, its, means, name, the, three
6	and, had, long, one, two
7	big, feet, were
8	animal, any, has, head, land, lived, of, on, that
9	be, could
10	a, plant, was
11	along, it
12	food, like, to, used
14	four, moved
15	back, than
16	near
17	in, part
18	about, from, more, out, people, years
20	can, go, learn, see

Page	Content Words First Appearance
5	Triceratops (pronounced: try-SAIR-uh-tops)
6	horns
10	eater
11	ground
12	beak, mouth
14	legs
16	lakes, ponds
17	North America
18	fossils
20	museums